SHAPES
IN GOD'S WORLD

written by
Beverly Beckmann

illustrated by
Kathy Mitter

Publishing House
St. Louis

Copyright © 1984 Concordia Publishing House
3558 S. Jefferson Avenue, St. Louis, MO 63118-3968
Manufactured in the United States of America

All rights reserved. No part of this publication may be reproduced, stored in a retrieval system, or transmitted, in any form or by any means, electronic, mechanical, photocopying, recording, or otherwise, without the prior written permission of Concordia Publishing House.

In the beginning God made all things.

Or we can tell about the things in God's world.

Sometimes we need a name to tell about God's world.

then the name of that shape is **circle**.

If it has four sides and four corners the same like the edge shapes on the turtle's shell,

if it has four sides and four corners the same like the stones around the farmer's home,

then the name of that shape is square.

if it has three sides the same like the web of the spider,

if it has three sides the same like the distant mountains,

then the name of that shape will be **triangle.**

If it has a body and a head,
if it has eyes, ears, a mouth and a nose,

then its name will be _____.
And God made all shapes, all things, and YOU.

Dear Family Members,

    Children come into contact with the basic shapes found in God's world every day of their lives. We can help them learn the names of these shapes and understand their characteristics through simple activities. This can be done by having the child look around the home or neighborhood for each shape. Also, cut shapes out of sandpaper or Styrofoam so that the coarse texture can be felt by the child. Then cut the basic shapes out of cardboard and have the child draw around the shapes.

    Children should understand that all things have names. We can describe an object's characteristics, but it does have a name. If it is round, it is called circle.

    People are God's creation too. They have characteristics, and they have names. In a child's eyes the most important name is its own. Have him or her place that name in the blank provided and explain that the name and the child are very special creations of God.